TAG–TEAM
YOUTH MINISTRY

50 Ways to Involve Parents and Other Caring Adults

FOREWORD BY **WAYNE RICE**

TAG-TEAM YOUTH MINISTRY

50 WAYS TO INVOLVE PARENTS AND OTHER CARING ADULTS

BY RON HABERMAS AND DAVID OLSHINE

Illustrated by Keith Locke

Standard Publishing
Cincinnati, Ohio

Dedication

We lovingly dedicate this book to our life-long "tag-team" partners in marriage and ministry, Mary and Rhonda. Thanks for your unswerving faithfulness "in our corner."

Cover Illustration by Keith Locke
Edited by Dale Reeves

Library of Congress Cataloging-in-Publication Data

Habermas, Ronald T.
    Tag-team youth ministry : 50 practical ways to involve parents and other caring adults / by Ron Habermas and David Olshine : illustrated by Keith Locke.
        p.   cm.
    ISBN 0-7847-0407-4
    1. Church work with youth. 2. Group ministry. 3. Christian education of teenagers. 4. Family--Religious life. I. Olshine, David, 1954- . II. Title.
BV4447.H293 1995
259'.23--dc20   95-8625
                                                                            CIP

The Standard Publishing Company, Cincinnati, Ohio
A Division of Standex International Corporation

02 01 00 99 98 97 96 95   5 4 3 2 1

Contents

PART 1   A New Game Plan for
             21st Century Youth
             Ministry   9

PART 11   50 Practical Strategies
             for Tag-Team Youth
             Ministry   33

PART 111 A Look in the
             Rearview Mirror   93

FOREWORD

Youth ministry is growing up. During its infancy (the 1950s and 60s) it cried out for attention and got it. In childhood (the 60s and 70s), it spent most of its time playing games. Nobody took it too seriously. As an adolescent (the 70s and 80s), it made a lot of noise, separated from the church, established an identity of its own and became "cool." As a young adult (the 80s and 90s), it got extremely busy and became quite successful.

Now, having reached a kind of "mid-life" (the 90s and beyond), youth ministry is going through a period of reassessment. Veteran youth workers are asking, "What are we really accomplishing?" and "Where do we need to go from here?"

My friends, Ron Habermas and David Olshine, have been asking questions like these for quite some time. In this book, they have provided some solid answers. They believe that the only good youth ministry is one that is done within the context of the family—the nuclear family and the extended family of God, the church. They use a marvelous image from the world of sports to describe this approach—the "tag team." No longer can youth work be done by a single youth worker, or even a youth ministry staff. It must involve the whole church, working together as a team.

Most importantly, it must involve parents. We who have been involved in youth ministry for more than a few years now know this is true: **Without parental support, the likelihood of a teen continuing in the faith as an adult is reduced significantly.** We may be able to get kids to come to our meetings and activities, and even get them to read their Bibles and behave themselves for a few years. But our ultimate goal in youth ministry is not just to have a successful youth group. It is, as Paul put it, to "present everyone perfect in Christ" (Colossians 1:28). Our objective is to someday see our youth following and serving Christ as adults.

That's why the tag-team approach is so important. Our kids need more than an exciting youth group. They need a dependable support system that will be there for them when the going gets rough. They need adult mentors who will provide them with the kind of guidance and encouragement they need to make good choices. They need a sense of significance as part of the body of Christ. In short, they need the church.

This is a great book. It is both thoughtful and practical. Read it and pay special attention to what the authors have to say about mentoring, community-building and the church as a "city of refuge." Better yet, put some of their ideas into practice and watch your youth ministry grow up.

Wayne Rice
Co-founder of Youth Specialties
Director of "Understanding Your Teenager" Seminars

PART 1

A New Game Plan
for 21st Century
Youth Ministry

CHAPTER 1—THE ANCIENT MODEL OF YOUTH MINISTRY: DIVIDE AND CONQUER

Adolescence, strictly speaking, is both a recent phenomenon (the term is about a century old) and a Western one. Traditionally, people matured straight from childhood to adulthood. Rites of passage, like the bar mitzvah and the bat mitzvah in Jewish cultures, for instance, typically ushered kids into adult realms of responsibility. There was no in-between stage.

In the "olden days" of the 1960s and early 1970s, three traits characterized youth work. First, **it focused on kids only.** We saw just one person—the teen. "Don't mess with parents," youth workers were told. Or, so we believed. This myth also claimed that adults were the concern of the senior pastor. Certainly not trained youth leaders.

Second, **all work was directed solely to youth.** Every strategy targeted them. Take counseling, for instance. We directed our full attention and plans to the kids. Not to parents. Certainly not to both—as families. When a student had a problem, whom did you counsel? "I need to talk with you," teens would say. And, the simple thing was to comply. Anything more than that seemed unnecessary. A kid had a problem. You brought her in, and you counseled according to the ancient model—one-on-one. You listened to her and then said, "I'm really sorry about that." After your meeting, you sent her back to her same unchanged environment. Three weeks later, she was messed up—again. And the cycle was the same for every counseling case. Kids came back and you tried to fix them up, again. But you sent them right back to the very same dysfunctional systems.

Or, remember this scenario? The youth went on a retreat. Some became Christians; others rededicated their lives. They were pumped up! Alive, on fire! You all came back and these rejuvenated youth reentered their unchanged families. What happened within a couple of days or weeks? They caved in. They reverted to their old patterns of behavior because the system was so strong—and so unchanged.

Third, in the ancient model, **youth work neglected parents of teenagers.** The word "avoidance" is too strong, perhaps. But not neglect. Whether conscious or not, parents were forgotten. Most of us youth workers were not trained to work with parents, but their kids. Ironically, if communication took place at all, it was initiated by them, not us! No news was good news: If youth workers didn't hear any disgruntled remarks, things must be OK on the home front.

Unfortunately, this ancient model is still alive and well today. And, sometimes, the youth worker is not the one keeping it alive. Uncooperative church leaders, threatened pastors and untrusting parents have each perpetuated the conventional patterns of this "Divide and Conquer" scheme —to separate teens from the very adult caregivers who could help them grow. But, more critical than the issue of who's to blame is the reality of spoils of this warfare—**teens always come out the losers.**

Somewhere in the early or middle 1970s, a major shift in youth ministry slowly began. This shift moved the focus from the **individual** teen to the teen **within the family.**

CHAPTER 2—Focus on the Family

As we turned the corner, in the mid-70s—towards the teen-in-the-family—a new vista appeared. New possibilities. But also, quite frankly, new limitations and problems.

But first, the good news. What did this new mind-set of "families" do for youth work? It assumed a new wide-angle view of youth ministry. That is, in comparison with the "ancient model," we workers took a **new perspective.** A broader vision. We realized that Scripture recognizes that kids are just one piece of the puzzle. They're only a small slice of the larger pie called the family. Children (and, there-fore, youth) are never separated from the larger reality and the significance of the home. This was a given throughout the Scripture. Even in our contemporary scene those who, for example, value the social services of orphanages always note that the nuclear family will never be replaced. Technically, this sociological-psychological viewpoint (which researches the influence and responsibility of the home in teen culture) is often called "Family Systems."

Second, in contrast to the ancient approach to youth, Scripture took a **new posture** when families were reintro-duced into the equation. Youth workers typically perceived themselves as assistants to the parents, as the parents directly ministered to their own kids. In other words, our new job reflected a more submissive stance. We empow-ered mom or dad to do what Proverbs 22:6 says—to help **them** train up **their** child in the way he or she should go. We were not called to be the parents. To state it differently, we were to minister like Barnabas, to be encouragers of parents. We stood behind the scenes. Theoretically, we helped them do what God had called them to do. At least, that's how it looked on paper.

Third, the new familial approach called for a **new part-nership.** We no longer viewed parents as adversaries. We did still have an enemy, as the Bible says, and his name is Satan. But flesh-and-blood parents were **not** our foes. They were our allies.

From time to time, however, we'd hear youth pastors cry out, "Yeah, but you don't understand **my** situation. You don't know the kind of parents I'm stuck with!" And it was true. We didn't know. But, no matter how bad it was, parents were still—technically—on our side. And, we were on theirs. We were both accountable to God for their teen's growth, at some level of accountability.

But then the cries got louder. And stronger. Early on, it was somewhat easier to ignore extreme complaints of dysfunctionality. (If nothing else, that word didn't even exist, in its current, notorious sense). Cries of abuse initially seemed the exception to the rule; then more were heard. Pandora's box was opened.

Beyond such unfortunate, extreme cases, other rumblings about the "family model" grabbed our attention: Parents didn't have the time to do what it took to raise mature Christian teens. They didn't have the Bible knowledge, either; polls continued to show us the startling rise of biblical illiteracy, even among churched household members. Furthermore, parents admitted they didn't have all the skills necessary to train their teens (how to understand teen culture and resources, how to communicate and how to instill internalized values).

Youth leaders were forced to go back to the drawing board. Back to Scripture. Down on their knees.

Indeed, families were found to be an important institution for youth work—the very first one, in fact, that God had blessed. But by focusing on the family almost exclusively, other biblical and sociological issues were neglected. Even more bad news was on the horizon.

CHAPTER 3—THE RISE AND FALL OF THE TRADITIONAL FAMILY

Just as the emphases began to focus on the teen-within-the-family—a significant pendulum swing in many youth ministries—the very definitions of the family were put up for grabs. Our society became unsure of what a family looked like. For years, influential leaders said the traditional family was a husband, a wife, two kids, a dog, a cat and a squirrel. But, with the present generation, anything goes. Single people say, "I thought I was a part of the traditional family." Divorced people say, "I don't get it. I thought I was part of the traditional family." Even homosexual partners describe themselves by this phrase. Our generation can't agree on an acceptable definition.

Nobody can deny that **something** has happened to the family during these past few years. In the least, such prominent shifts in definitions have caused confusion. Many people, especially in the church, have labeled such recent changes with even stronger terms; words like "failure," "decline," even the old-fashioned word, "sin," have been reintroduced.

The bottom line is that our teens in this generation are caught in this mess. What was "abnormal" to **us** during this shift in definitions has become "normal" to **them.** Our youth know of no other model or pattern. These "new" definitions are all they know. They're the ones that are caught in this cross fire of pain, immorality and injustice.

Divorce, for example, has become an easy option. Studies in certain sectors of society show that as many as one out of two persons that get married will get divorced. And the church is hardly immune to such statistics. In fact, one of the most pressing ministries in many megachurches today is divorce recovery. How many of the teens that we work with come from broken homes? Their unending stories of hurt, betrayal, disillusionment and doubt are incredible.

Single-parent homes are, therefore, on the rise. These households are usually headed by women, which often creates the additional stressors of inadequate income and unbalanced gender role modeling. Blended families are also emerging. Just look at a roster of names in your youth group. It's not unusual anymore for one of your teens to be called by certain legal names this week that he didn't even have last week! It's not uncommon to discover an adolescent in your group who lives with two adults, neither of whom are her natural parents.

And, what's our reaction to all this confusion? How should we respond? Minimally, **we must become more aware.** We must become sensitive to who's "out there" in the teen groups we serve. We must frequently remind ourselves (and others) of these sociological shifts that have taken place. We must regularly look in the mirror and say: "Hello, youth worker! Wake up and smell the coffee! Wake up to twenty-first century youth ministry!"

We also need to be cautious of our presumptions—specifically our presumptions that "families are stable," "families are mature" and "families are strong." We must admit that, in some cases, individual teens are more mature than their family leaders. But, we need more than a simple response of awareness and rejection of presumptions. Much more. These are **reactive** responses. They come after the fact. It's rearview-mirror mentality, always looking to the past. That's okay, initially, but there's a greater challenge.

We must be **proactive,** too. We must have a game plan that is preventative (vs. corrective), that anticipates (vs. knee-jerks) and that looks ahead (vs. looks behind). To accomplish this task, we must address at least three issues:

1. **What insight does Scripture offer?**
2. **Is there an even better model of youth ministry—better than a focus on the teen alone or on the teen within the family?**
3. **What practical help can we use immediately?**

CHAPTER 4—LET'S START AT THE VERY BEGINNING: BIBLICAL INSIGHTS

Most youth ministries get sidetracked because their purpose is unsure. Often, workers are so caught up in programs or promoting someone else's agenda that they fail to see the big picture. They forget to identify **why** they do **what** they do. When that happens—and it usually does—disaster is to be expected. The workers can never assess their Christian service. They never know if they're getting closer to their goal and reasons for ministry.

Let's start at the very beginning. Start with Scripture . . . again. What should our objective be for youth work? Many suggestions have been offered, regarding the overarching purposes of youth work—things like "to love God," "to glorify God" and "to mature in Christ."

These are all well and good, but we would like to suggest a new concept: **the ultimate goal of reconciliation.** I [Ron] have discussed this concept, in great detail, as an educational model for all ages (see TEACHING FOR RECONCILIATION, Baker Books, 1992; coauthored with Klaus Issler).

In brief, the biblical concept of "reconciliation" means to "reunite" and "to make whole again." Perhaps the best passage of Scripture on this challenge to wholeness is 2 Corinthians 5:17—6:1. There, the apostle Paul tells us that God "reconciled us to himself through Christ." Also, he subsequently "gave us the ministry of reconciliation." Finally, "he has committed to us the message of reconciliation." It sounds like Paul is repeating himself, but, really, he's trying to make sure his point comes across.

Think of it as something that "all the king's horses and all the king's men" could not do for Humpty Dumpty—to "put him together again." **We must help teens become whole.** That's it. That's our ultimate job.

If we would break down this enormous, lifelong task of

reconciliation, we would discover four prominent subgoals:
- the need to reconcile each teen **to God**
- the need to reconcile each teen **to himself**
- the need to reconcile each teen **to other believers**
- the need to reconcile each teen **to his or her calling in life**

Figure 1 (page 19) identifies these same four subgoals, respectively, in these terms: **communion, character, congregation** and **commission.** Each of these terms match up with specific issues of human development, in particular: faith, moral, social and vocational development concerns. Each area marks an important part of youth work.

We find these four subgoals best represented in Acts 2:42-47, concerning God's powerful work in the early church. First, communion is stressed through the believers' "prayer" (v. 42) and praise (v. 47). Second, character is noted by the saints' devotion to the "apostles' teaching" (v. 42), which prompted individual knowledge and growth. Third, congregation issues are emphasized in that believers were "devoted . . . to the fellowship" (v. 42). Furthermore, two practical examples of their communal love in the church are evidenced by the fact that they were "together and had everything in common" (v. 44). And, fourth, the subgoal of commission is cited because the early church reached out to serve its larger constituency. The believers had a great reputation in their neighborhoods, for they were "selling their possessions" and "they gave to anyone as he had need" (v. 45). These are marks of mature ministry accomplishments.

What's the purpose of youth work, then? **Making teens whole**, in every sense. If we see signs of growth in any one of the four subgoals, we have succeeded in youth work.

Figure 1.
"Big Picture" Understanding of Purpose

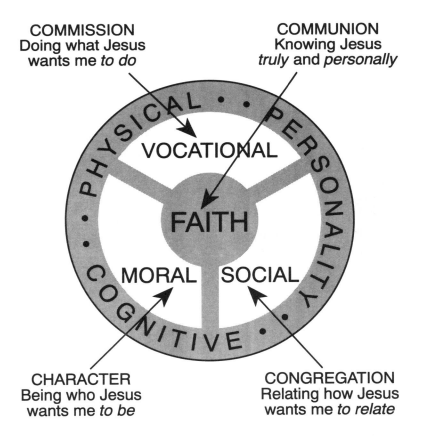

COMMISSION
Doing what Jesus
wants me *to do*

COMMUNION
Knowing Jesus
truly and *personally*

PHYSICAL · · PERSONALITY

VOCATIONAL

FAITH

MORAL SOCIAL

COGNITIVE ·

CHARACTER
Being who Jesus
wants me *to be*

CONGREGATION
Relating how Jesus
wants me *to relate*

By D. Rahn. Adapted from Habermas & Issler, TEACHING FOR RECONCILIATION, Baker Books, 1992.

CHAPTER 5—IS THERE A BETTER MODEL?

To review, then, in the 60s and early 70s, youth ministry focused on the **individual teen.** Youth workers were seen as surrogate godparents. Youth pastors—often Lone Ranger types—served as spiritual gurus. They were viewed as the expert—expert Bible study leader, expert games-meister and expert fund-raiser. In short, expert "center-stage" person.

By the mid-70s the shift began to include **the teen within-the-family.** This new emphasis on the home meant that roles changed, too. Youth workers were expected to be Big Brothers and Sisters. Youth pastors became advisers or counselors, since bringing parents and siblings into the picture usually involved both formal and informal get-togethers, discussing such matters as discipline, responsibility and effective communication. Although the initiative for most ministries still came from the youth pastor's office, this professional often took a "behind-the-scenes" position. It was almost an overreaction to the previous "center-stage" position.

Now, in the 90s, the pendulum is swinging again. The new focus is on **community.** By far the most comprehensive of the three emphases, this new model values the teen as individual, the teen in the family, and the teen within the larger scope of his or her environment. Based upon a broader look at Scripture and other significant studies, youth work has taken a quantum leap. A whole new dimension. Various members of the neighborhood-at-large are perceived to be part of the successful teen equation: parents, educators, law enforcement officers, community leaders, staff and volunteers of youth-serving organizations, churches and even businesses.

In one study by Search Institute, approximately 47,000 students in grades 6-12 were surveyed. They represented 111 communities and 25 states. Among other conclusions, Search found that multiple deficits within the surveyed youth (such as overexposure to TV or physical abuse) often led to at-risk behavior (e.g., use of alcohol, depression, etc.). Conversely, strong youth assets (like concern for others or educational aspirations) significantly reduced at-risk behavior.

Consider the following list of fourteen assets that this particular study recommended to promote a resilient response to at-risk behavior—how teens can be inoculated against harmful conduct, so to speak. Simply, the more that these fourteen qualities exist in a teen's life, the healthier his or her development will be.

Search discovered it's everyone's job to pitch in and help youth to mature. Specifically note the wide range of people, groups and organizations that are being called upon to help, based on these fourteen assets; make a mental list of volunteers and professionals in your neighborhood who could help in these areas:

- **Church/synagogue involvement**
- **School extracurricular activities**
- **Community clubs and organizations**
- **Parental standards**
- **Parental discipline**
- **Achievement motivation**
- **Educational aspirations**
- **Homework**
- **Helping people values**
- **Concern for poor**
- **Sexual restraint**
- **Family support**
- **Parent(s) as social resources**
- **School climate**

With this new **community** model, youth workers basically become responsible community members, doing their particular part as contributors to the comprehensive process of teen maturity. Youth pastors serve the role of advocate, within a wide range of professionals and volunteers in their specific community. In addition, they themselves offer their own specialized assistance to teen growth.

The community model, then, reflects a more complex and sophisticated picture—both of the problems of youth ministry and of the solutions. **It's critical to notice, therefore, that earlier emphases of youth work are not supposed to be dismissed or abandoned.** Rather, they are purposefully included and expanded, through this new, preferred community model. In other words, no longer should teens be seen as merely isolated individuals, nor are they and their families to be viewed as purely separate entities from other outside influences.

These former emphases, indeed, have their place, but a larger landscape must be painted. That landscape features the larger community. It's intentionally intergenerational; intentionally "extended family."[1]

Figure 2 illustrates how these three teen emphases interact.

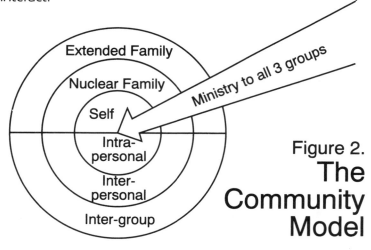

Figure 2.
The Community Model

---

[1] For further biblical study of the intergenerational "community model," consider these passages: Acts 4:32-37; 1 Timothy 3:4, 5; 4:11-14; 5:1-16; 2 Timothy 1:3-7; 2:2, 22, 23; 3:14, 15; Titus 2:1-8; and James 1:27.

A mentor is someone who offers skills to someone else—skills that person does not have himself. Mentors are needed at all levels of teen work, just as the apostle Paul declared in his writings:

1. Mentors for individual teens

- A mentor should be a spiritual leader (2 Timothy 2:2)
- A mentor should be a mature adult who has been influential to the child (now a teen) for several years (2 Timothy 3:14, 15)
- A mentor should be a mature individual teen ("peer leader") who lives righteously and uses his or her gift (1 Timothy 4:11-14)

2. Mentors for youth-within-families

- Spiritual leadership is a requirement of those who want to be overseers in the church (1 Timothy 3:4, 5)
- Mentors are godly parents and grandparents (2 Timothy 1:3-7; 3:14, 15)

3. Mentors for youth-in-community

- Intergenerational mentoring is expected in a healthy Christian environment (1 Timothy 5:1, 2; Titus 2:1-8)

Okay, now what? What should be done to implement the community model? What practical strategies can be suggested? What paradigms are needed?

CHAPTER 6—THREE
BIBLICAL STRATEGIES

How do we, in practical terms, combine the biblical principles of our purpose (reconciliation and its four subgoals) with the new plan of community? Three biblical strategies come to mind. They represent useful, organizational vehicles through which purpose and plan come together.

Each strategy represents **balance,** because this threesome offers a stable diet for health and growth. Each strategy also represents **harmony,** for the focus on the individual teen, the focus on the teens in families and the focus on communities complement one another. These areas never negate or duplicate ministry to teens, as shown below.

The first biblical strategy, then, is the need for **centers of worship and instruction.** Like believers in the Old and New Testaments, teens today must have consistent opportunities for praise and nurture. Besides other benefits, this strategy offers the balance component of inward growth. Centers of worship and instruction rejuvenate the soul and spirit, while replenishing the mind. Harmony is demonstrated by promoting worship and instruction in the home and by emphasizing worship and instruction in the community of faith, as well. The failure of one of these institutions to uphold its responsibility to teens does not negate the other institution's duty; nor does the successful accomplishment of one make the other one's service redundant. Both are necessary; each affirms the other.

The second biblical plan is the need for **sites of celebration.** In both Testaments, this strategy is featured via festivals, such as Passover. These celebrations called for reflection and rejoicing, for recall and recommitment. As then, so now, the balance element of upward growth is highlighted. Time schemes of past, present and future are purposely linked in these annual festivities; vertical relationships between creature and Creator are empowered and recharged. Contemporary teen ministry finds harmony, at the congregational level, through meaningful ordinances of the Lord's Supper and baptism. Harmony, on the home front, can represent faith festivals through family reunions, holiday gatherings and even informal get-togethers. Faith-in-life, in order to be effective, must be experienced in a variety of places and events.

The third biblical strategy points to a few rather obscure references in the Old Testament. It is based upon the historical call for **cities of refuge.** Since this final strategy is least known, a bit more detail will be provided.

Back in Joshua's day, God commanded that six literal cities in the promised land be designated as "cities of refuge." Their primary purpose was to serve as a sanctuary, a haven of freedom, for the person who accidentally killed someone. This runaway—fleeing those who would naturally want to avenge the victim—was to receive a fair trial and subsequent protection, in one of these half-dozen locations.

Notice God's command for these cities, from Joshua 20:1-9: "Then the LORD said to Joshua: 'Tell the Israelites to designate the cities of refuge, as I instructed you through Moses, so that anyone who kills a person accidentally and unintentionally may flee there and find protection from the avenger of blood.

'When he flees to one of these cities, he is to stand in the entrance of the city gate and state his case before the elders of that city. Then they are to admit him into their city and give him a place to live with them. If the avenger of blood pursues him, they must not surrender the one accused, because he killed his neighbor unintentionally and without malice aforethought. He is to stay in that city until he has stood trial before the assembly and until the death of the high priest who is serving at that time. Then he may go back to his own home in the town from which he fled.'

So they set apart Kedesh in Galilee in the hill country of Naphtali, Shechem in the hill country of Ephraim, and Kiriath Arba (that is, Hebron) in the hill country of Judah. On the east side of the Jordan of Jericho they designated Bezer in the desert on the plateau in the tribe of Reuben, Ramoth in Gilead in the tribe of Gad, and Golan in Bashan in the tribe of Manasseh. Any of the Israelites or any alien living among them who killed someone accidentally could flee to these designated cities and not be killed by the avenger of blood prior to standing trial before the assembly."

Teens, today, figuratively take the role of the refugee. They face incredible stressors and an unprecedented pressure from the outside world—comparable to the innocent victim of old, who was relentlessly pursued by an avenger. What a powerful image the city of refuge provides us!

A commendable goal of every youth worker in the twenty-first century is to equip parents to provide symbolic cities of refuge in their homes, for their teens. Also, by way of harmony, youth workers must encourage leaders in the faith community to, likewise, protect and serve their teens. Employing this strategy as a metaphor will yield a half-dozen principles from Scripture.

First, cities of refuge must be **visible.** Historically, at least five of these six cities were located in the hill country or on plateaus. That is, they were selected, in part, to be seen from a distance. Symbolically interpreted, this means that the contemporary home and church must be public and evident to all. They must be ready to serve their members. They must be visible and able to do what good homes and congregations do—nurture.

Second, as cities of refuge, families and faith communities should be **approachable.** Deuteronomy 19:2, 3 states that the Israelites were to "build roads to [these cities]." This was a highly unusual command for that day, given the cities' location in the high country. Parents in the contemporary home must symbolically build roads of accessibility. Leaders in the church must construct similar pathways. This means that effective tag-team youth ministries recruit adult care-givers who are willing to be present for teenagers' needs. "Roads" of availability, good listening and friendly communication must be paved; and they must be regularly maintained and repaired.

Third, youth ministry is committed to linking arms with families and the community to promote **hospitality.** Someone once defined the home as "a place to go to fail safely." Hospitality means that we must turn our homes and local fellowships into hospitals—to mend the hurting, to heal the sick. This call for hospitality reaches beyond the confines of its own membership. Teens who live in the home—but also their friends—are privileged to receive such humane treatment. The church must likewise put out the welcome mat—especially for unchurched teens or inactive youth.

Joshua 20:9 recognizes that these cities were to serve "Israelites or any alien [i.e., a non-Israelite]." There was to be no prejudice; no bias. Joshua 20:4 adds that the elders of these select sites were to meet such runaways at "the entrance of the city gate" and then to "give [them] a place to live with them." Now, that's hospitality!

Fourth, cities of refuge were to be **protective.** Numbers 35:9ff. admonishes city leaders to support those who committed these life-taking crimes unintentionally. Then, verse twenty-five broadens this command, stating, "the assembly must protect the one accused." For twenty-first century youth ministry, the word "assembly" is particularly significant. We workers must help our church leaders and volunteers to answer the question: "How are you protecting those kids 'within your gates'?" Unfortunately, part of that protection means that we must be a haven for those who have suffered physical abuse. Besides physical protection, do your teens feel secure emotionally, psychologically and spiritually? That is, do they sense an environment of trust? Can they freely raise any issue they want—even doubts about their faith—without feeling threatened?

Fifth, contemporary youth ministries need to assist parents and community believers to **be fair.** Unfairness is a double-edged sword: oftentimes, we leaders either jump to conclusions, on one hand, or we overlook wrongdoings, on the other hand. Against that backdrop, prudent leaders will counter these imbalances by providing the benefit of the doubt (i.e., not judging teens prematurely) and by exhibiting "tough love," respectively. Cities of refuge were to offer fair trials to all runaways. They were never to be characterized by injustice.

Sixth and finally, when it comes to serving its teens, parents and congregational members must be **selfless.** Joshua 20:6 records that the final purpose of these cities was to, eventually, have the refugee "go back to his own home in the town from which he fled." Symbolically, this means "letting go" of our teens. This gradual process must start when the teenager is young. We youth workers should assist all who influence youth by helping them include these young teens in various decisions, by teaching them individual responsibility and by instilling in them the goal of social interdependence—a healthy give-and-take between every mature believer.

Cities of refuge provide the balance of outward growth, since noble virtues of a safe haven and a fair trial for "outsiders" are secured.

In summary, if today's teens could experience these three strategies of balance, they would grow—individually, within the home and within the community of faith—through worship and instruction; celebration and recommitment; and safety and justice.

CHAPTER 7—A NEW AND IMPROVED MODEL: COMMUNITY

Recent history has shown that the ancient model of youth ministry eventually short-circuits. It self-destructs. Ironically, the teens who are supposed to be the exclusive focus are the ultimate losers. Biblically speaking, the ancient model has no future, either.

The family model approach to youth work also has its problems. In fact, this chapter is for those who might need to be more convinced that teen ministry must not rely solely upon the family model. Specifically, there are at least three hurdles that challenge youth workers, when they see parents as allies—especially if they see them as their **only** allies.

First, in working with familial caregivers, we need to realize that **many parents are emotionally distant.** I [David] was once doing a parent-teen seminar. It was going to be a fun and crazy night.

We'd informed all the parents about this. So, as I was coming out of the church building on the morning of this big event, I saw one of the girls in our youth group with her dad. (I found out much later that she came from a dysfunctional family with a lot of abuse. But I didn't know it, since she was the kind of kid that always came to every youth event. Later, I realized that our youth group was the only place where she felt safe. In fact, it was her home.) So, as I saw her with her dad, I said to him, "Hi! How are you?" He kind of mumbled, and I turned to her and asked, "Are you coming to our event tonight?" And he shouted, "No!" I reacted, "I'd really like both of you to come." Silence. Then I inquired, "Do you mind me asking why you don't want to come?" (You know what they say: "Fools rush in . . ."). He responded, "I just don't want to come; I'm busy." As he left, his daughter confessed, "I'm really sorry." I assured her it wasn't her fault. Later, it dawned on me that many parents are emotionally distant. They are often oblivious to what's going on in their teens' lives. They're isolated. They're clueless about what God wants for them and for their kids. It's more than ignorance. It's aloofness. It's cold.

Secondly, **many parents feel powerless.** What happens to us when we feel powerless? We often become defensive. Or, we become angry. We may attack what we perceive to be our enemy. Or, we disengage. Whatever the response, the result is the same: unproductive behavior. Parents feel powerless because they believe that with the first sign of puberty—with the first hormonal surge—their formerly innocent child becomes an uncontrollable monster. It's a terrible myth that darkens these years of parenthood. Where once good communication might have existed between adult and child, now—almost overnight—a wall is erected. And, the funny thing is that this barrier is often solely constructed by the adult in the family.

The third and last challenge in working with adults in the home is that **many parents bring their own set of baggage.** They bring their own problems, their own ignorance and their own immaturity. Often these problems are passed on to their kids, just like genetic traits. A family model to youth ministry, for example, tells us that if mom or dad has a temper that was never controlled, the kids are likely to, as well. In part, it's what Exodus 34:7 means when it says that the "sin of the fathers" will be passed on to their children's children "to the third and fourth generation." You've heard teenagers say, "I'm not going to be like mom or dad." But, unless they break sinful and unproductive patterns, they will parent like them. We're all creatures of imitation.

The flip side of parents' baggage is the youth leader's baggage. To make the most of this model, veteran youth worker Paul Borthwick says that we need to claim a new mind-set. We must overcome what he calls **"Parentnoia"**— a paranoia of parents. There are four specific, common feelings of anxiety that we must overcome. One anxiety is **fear.**

For example, let's say that Allison's mom and you had a serious disagreement about youth work. The next time you see her at church, what do you do? You avoid her. Fear freezes. It seizes you. You see her walking down the hall in the church building, and you exit stage right. Fear of encounter. Fear of confrontation.

We also have parentnoia based on **criticism.** You know, you're afraid that someone might have a better way of doing youth ministry than you. We don't like to hear that our ideas are second-rate. After all, we're the experts, aren't we? For example, what if a parent criticizes your mission trip by saying, "Hey, why did you leave my kid in Mexico?"

A related problem is **self-centeredness.** We think to ourselves, "I'm the youth worker. I know a lot more about Brad than his mom or dad do." We develop a cozy, egotistical frame of mind. As this happens, we isolate ourselves from parents. Rather than being available to parents, as a family systems model encourages, we stiff-arm them. And we say, "Why should I help them? They've never supported me!"

Finally, parentnoia breeds **insecurity.** If we are to partner with parents in ministry, how do we relate to them one-on-one? For instance, say you decide to take one of your parents out to lunch. You ask yourself, "How am I supposed to act? Like I'm buddy-buddy with his kid? Do I show up in a coat and tie? Do I tell the parent some things I know about his teen (that he might not like to hear) even after I'm certain I'm not breaking any confidences? What is my role as 'expert'? Will he be thinking, 'That's what we pay you for!'?"

When you start to jumble all that up in your mind, usually the result is insecurity. You waver and think, "Maybe I won't even involve parents. Maybe I'll just back off and work just with kids. It's easier just to do it all myself."

That's when a lot of prayer, reflection and good counsel is called for. If we're honest with ourselves, we discover that the family model is both biblical and practical. If we're going to impact junior high or high school students, then we

must somehow impact their families, too. We can't help a kid to change and, then, throw her back into an unchanged home environment. That's downright stupid—and unethical.

We have to assume that every family can damage the goods. That is, they can, at times, do more harm than good. They can't go it alone. We need each other in the church for quality control. All families—even solid ones— need a broader base of knowledge, giftedness, assistance and support. Buy into the idea that we must address more than part of the system (the family). The whole system (the entire community of faith) should be acknowledged.

So, when you think about teen ministry in this light, consider something else. There are probably two kinds of youth workers who are reading these pages along with you: those who are tracking with the family model and those who've shifted to the community model. Who knows, there may be those who are still operating by the ancient model.

Regardless of where you are, the next section is for you. It gets you thinking about **practical ideas** for tag-team youth ministry. It strongly suggests that you shouldn't go it alone—whatever model you've tuned into. It says you need collective assistance. Cooperation. Others to lean on.

It says, "Take a breath. Here are a couple of fresh ideas to consider. Ponder them. Pray about them. Try them out."

The first half of practical strategies **(numbers 1-23)** focuses on involving parents directly; **numbers 24-50** also include community ideas; for parents and other adults in the congregation. See these ideas as suggestions to promote successful youth ministry. Read that line again. These are "suggestions," not final "solutions." They are points of beginning, not ways to conclude your work with kids.

So look at them in this light. Modify them. Tweak them. Radically change them. Or come up with your own. Be a risk taker. But do **something.** Something is better than nothing. Do something to help your teens. Do something to help their parents. Do something to help God's kingdom.

PART 11

50

Practical Strategies for Tag-Team Youth Ministry

Hold Parent Information Meetings

The purpose of a parent meeting is to inform about upcoming youth group events. This could be done once a year, but once a quarter is ideal. What do you do at these meetings? A variety of possibilities exist. They could take the form of an "open house," especially if you're coming in as a new staff person, or if they're new to you. Keep the meeting brief and lively. Let them get to know each other. Begin with a crowdbreaker and sing a song or two.

Briefly describe your philosophy of ministry. Or, say something about what you'll be doing, like: "During Spring Break, we're going skiing. This summer we're heading to Mexico to serve the poor. We also plan to have four major retreats during the year and three fund-raisers." If possible, give parents dates and costs four to six months in advance. The key is to keep a pattern of communication alive—a pattern that you're modeling for them to emulate in return.

2 CREATE A PARENT NEWSLETTER

Strive to put it out four to six times a year. Now, you're probably saying to yourself at this point, "Even if these fifty ideas are fantastic, this is a lot of extra work for me. . . . I'm already behind!" But listen to my [David's] story.

I prayed for God to bring someone to me who would take this newsletter on, precisely because I didn't have the time to do it. Within two weeks, a young woman came to my door. Her name was Liz. She said, "David, I would like to be involved in the youth ministry, but I have some problems." I responded, "What are your problems?" Liz stated, "Well, first of all, I don't like teenagers. Secondly, I'm not that organized, so I don't want to go on retreats. I don't want to go on any kind of trips." I said, "Well, those **do** limit some aspects of youth work. What are you interested in?" Liz countered, "Well, I was the editor for my high school newspaper." And I reacted, "Bingo! I've got just the job for you!" And so, four times a year, Liz collected pictures, interviewed people and put the newsletter together. She loved C.S. Lewis, so the newsletters were plastered with his quotes.

A word of advice: Make it a newsletter for parents. Mail it to **them.** Why? Because, when you send a teenager a newsletter, it goes in the wastebasket. Guaranteed. Send it to the parents if you want your newsletter read.

3 CREATE A PARENTS' PRAYER CHAIN

Encourage partnerships with parents by inviting them to join smaller subgroups of prayer. These can be organized by geographical location, by topic or theme. It's wise to have a responsible parent serve as the coordinator of each group. This coordinator begins the prayer chain, calling the prayer request on to the next person on her list. To check for efficiency and to promote accountability, the last person of the chain calls the coordinator back. Limit the size of each group to six people. Utilize as many parents who **really** want to pray. This is not meant for all adults; don't make them feel that it is.

4 ☙ START A MINI-SERIES

Keep this instruction just four to six weeks long. Use something like the video series by Wayne Rice and Ken Davis, called, UNDERSTANDING YOUR TEENAGER[2]. You may want to narrow your audience to parents who have preteens. Even consider inviting parents of kids in the third and fourth grade. Why? These adults are nervous. They can feel puberty coming on their kids. They know it's around the next corner. Many of them are scared. Therefore, they need to be ready.

---

[2]Published by Youth Specialties/Zondervan, 1992.

5 BUILD SUPPORT STRUCTURES

There are some good resources in print, which encourage parents via small groups. Tim Smith's book, HI! I'M BOB AND I'M THE PARENT OF A TEENAGER[3], is great. It can be studied together in six to eight weeks. Also, Serendipity House produces several broad support group materials that are designed for seven weeks, or they can be expanded to thirteen weeks. It's not deep material intended only for a therapy group. The goal is to help parents remember their own teen years. These publications also enable caregivers to realize that their challenge is **not** unique with their kid.

---

[3]Published by Gospel Light, 1991.

6 SECURE THE HOME-FIELD ADVANTAGE

Make a visit to the house of the teen's parents. Your purpose is just to say, "Hi! I'm glad to see you, and I really appreciate your [son or daughter]." Get on their turf. It's a pastoral strategy. Meet them where they are. And, held in their home, it's a safe place for them. Parents will end up supporting you and your ministry in new ways.

⑦ BE A CUT-UP

Prepare a brief mailer for parents, highlighting what's hot in youth culture. Subscribe to YOUTHWORKER UPDATE[4], or other resources on trends. Be an ongoing student of contemporary youth culture. Clip and paste useful news items. Add photos of your youth group events. Personalize it. Write a short article on adolescent development. Send it to the parents. Sign your name. They'll think you're a genius.

---

[4]Published by Youth Specialties, Inc., 800-769-7624.

8 PLAN A "SUNDAY NIGHT OUT"

Send out a letter saying you're going to have an evening **for parents only.** Ask the church to provide baby-sitting (or have your students take care of this). Invite parents together just to talk informally. Ask, "What sort of issues are you personally dealing with?" You may want to show a video. Maybe have a case study.

Consider other resources (like David Lynn's PARENT MINISTRY TALKSHEETS[5]), which stimulate good communication. Les Parrott III, in his book, HELPING THE STRUGGLING ADOLESCENT[6], lists thirty problematic issues like anger, anorexia, bulimia and peer pressure. He identifies why the problem occurs, what the symptoms are and when to refer. Parrott has great case studies in every chapter. You could use those relevant to your parents.

---

[5]Published by Youth Specialties/Zondervan, 1992.
[6]Published by Zondervan, 1993.

9 ⚙ CREATE A CLASS ACT

Have a Sunday school class just for parents of youth. This could be done in a number of ways. Obviously, you could deal with issues pertinent for parents of teens. For example, Kevin Huggins has an excellent book and video called PARENTING ADOLESCENTS[7]. It's a super way to get parents talking about what's going on in the home between adults and teens.

Or, you could deal with other concerns in their lives. Study subjects pertaining to broader adult issues of personal faith and growth, using topical works by authors like Chuck Swindoll. That way, you don't always press the panic buttons of parenting; rather, you create natural networks for them. We don't just want to have reactive classes—responding to crises within their teens' lives. We need proactive classes—preventing immature behavior through constructive growth patterns.

---

[7]Published by NavPress, 1989.

"Focus on the Family," in Counseling and Other Ways

The previous section stressed the need for joint ministry, in contrast to traditional ways. To repeat, don't invite just the teen in. When a parent asks you to counsel his teenager, recognize that you might need to counsel parent and teen together. Sometimes by inviting the adolescent alone, we don't see the whole pie, but just a piece of it. But do more. Invite parents to specific youth group activities. When appropriate, encourage them to participate in various fund-raisers, mission trips and camps.

(11) Get Away From It All

Many youth ministries have begun to establish parent-teen retreats. If you've never done one, begin with a small step. Plan an evening event. Try a Saturday from 9-4, or just a morning session. You don't need to have a speaker or video to address parent-teen issues, although you could. Feel free to do something more informal—more hands-on. For instance, what would happen if parents and their teenagers learned to work together? Have a neighborhood project in which they can get their hands dirty.

Why not let them play together—on a ropes course? It's hysterical to see mom or dad stuck on these obstacles, and guess who helps them out? What a learning experience! You could have a scavenger hunt and let parent-teen teams look for things that characterize healthy family traits. When they return, talk about how these qualities pertain to **their** home scene.

Smart Scheduling

Remind parents of the need for them to plan ahead, by coordinating any dates that affect the youth ministry. For example, if the youth group is small enough, graduation parties and open houses for seniors could be organized with the church calendar of events, to avoid unnecessary conflicts. Requests for the use of church facilities, basketball games, birthday parties and Bible studies should be coordinated by a parent or adult volunteer.

If you want to send a message to parents that you really care about scheduling, cancel youth group on occasion. Call it "Off Night." Send a letter to explain your desire for teens and parents to have some family time together. Include a plethora of practical ideas for their night together. Radical? Yes, but one your parents will appreciate. (You might want to let your church leaders know beforehand—in case you want to keep your job.)

13 BE A ROVING REPORTER

With video recorder in hand, drop in on homes unannounced. With the tape rolling, ask questions like:

- **"What's for dinner?"**
- **"Has Shannon done her home-work yet?"**
- **"Can we see Scott's room, without anybody picking up before we get there?"**

Show these impromptu videos at the next youth gathering. It's a scream! If you have any creative filmmaker-wannabes in your group, have them splice in a few extras, such as youth group "commercials," to add some spice.

SPREAD THE GOOD NEWS AROUND

Have you ever had a teenager come to you and ask, "Would you write an endorsement letter for me, so I can be camp counselor next summer?" or, "so I can go on a mission trip?" or, "so I can attend college?" I [David] once did something that illustrates how this can be a great opportunity for ministry. Amy asked me for a recommendation to go on a mission trip with Teen Mania Ministries®. After I wrote the letter, I thought Amy's parents might like to know about it. So, I sent them a copy with this comment, "Mark and Paula, this is the note that I sent to Teen Mania Ministries® to tell them what a great kid Amy is." Three days later I got a phone call from the mom. "Thank you so much for showing you care," she said. This simple strategy is a great way of saying to parents, "I'm for you and I'm for your kid." Too many times parents never hear a word about their child, unless it's negative.

ORGANIZE A FAMILY OLYMPICS

Select a handful of families to compete against each other in a variety of games. Create replicas of the real thing: for example, instead of equestrian events, race tricycles through an obstacle course. Provide gold, silver and bronze medals. Bring your video camera and interview families concerning their preparation for the events, their strategies, etc. Sell tickets. Let the games begin!

 ## HONOR (THEIR) FATHERS AND MOTHERS

Start a "Parent-of-the-Month" Club. Honor those who go beyond the call of duty. Let kids make the nominations. Each month, photograph the winner, explain his or her noteworthy deeds and, then, spread the word. Post the news on a prominent bulletin board in the lobby. Announce their names in church services. Offer a gift certificate. Rejoice with them!

17 Establish Credit Card Mentality

Take at least one parent on every retreat, trip, mission trip or out-of-town event. That is, **"don't leave home without them."** Why? They have wisdom. They have experience. They offer you balance, by giving a different perspective. They'll also cover your back when things go wrong, like when your church bus breaks down and you arrive home three hours late. So, invite them on every trip you ever do, even if it's just twenty minutes away from the church. You'll be glad you did.

18 Go Down on Your Knees

Pray regularly for your parents. It's important because they have so many needs. Perhaps you can tie this task in with previous suggestions.

For example, have a hot-line number for them to call in a prayer request, or include a tear-off section in their newsletter. The key is to let them know you care, that you're available to serve them before the throne of God.

19 ORGANIZE A "COLLEGE FAIR DAY"

Parents—oftentimes, more than their kids— are anxious about issues pertaining to college. Schedule a special gathering of juniors, seniors and their parents to address this need. I [Ron] had a great time with this strategy: area representatives from various schools were invited to the church one night. They set up booths, handed out their propaganda and gave a few minutes of pep talk. Even though many college reps couldn't show up in person, they were more than willing to send a video, a slide presentation or just literature. The key for success is planning. Set a date far enough in advance for teens, their parents and area schools. You may want to advertise this event in your students' schools.

"For Juniors and Seniors Only" Meetings

Invite juniors and seniors to special gatherings. For example, for college-bound kids, discuss SAT testing, neighborhood tutoring programs and scholarship opportunities (even work-study opportunities—the blue-collar-type of scholarship). Bring in a local guidance counselor for a Q & A session.

Organize a Parent Seminar

ATTENTION: PARENTS OF TEENAGERS! HOW TO KEEP YOUR KIDS FROM MEETING ME! SGT. MARK DEEDS of the SPRINGFIELD POLICE

This could be done once or twice a year. Or, it could be done as many times as you have the energy and vision for. Invite someone in your community who is a first-rate communicator: a guidance counselor, a law enforcement officer, a teacher or a psychologist. This is a prime-time opportunity for reaching unchurched parents of teenagers. Just about any parent of any teenager wants to be better equipped to meet the needs of her child. Some possible subjects include: how to talk to your teenager about sex or how to listen to his hurts.

Publicize the event everywhere. This is a great "connector" to the leaders in your broader community. And, it's a super bridge to unchurched families.

22 CREATE A "WHAT'S NEXT?" SEMINAR

How do we help teens make necessary connections beyond high school? What issues will they face? How do faith and life merge for them? Invite these teens-in-transition and their caregivers to study pertinent issues together. For instance, Dr. James Dobson has just released an excellent seven-part video series entitled LIFE ON THE EDGE[8]. Titles include FINDING GOD'S WILL FOR YOUR LIFE, LOVE MUST BE TOUGH and WHEN GOD DOESN'T MAKE SENSE.

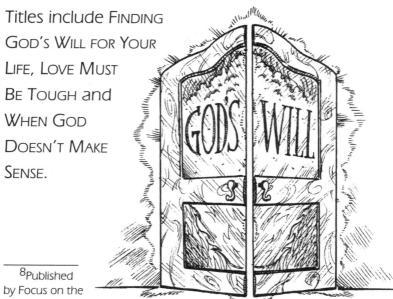

[8]Published by Focus on the Family, 1993.

 SAY "CHEESE"!

Every fall, get a responsible teen or adult to capture the year on film; through slides or videos. Specifically tell the individual to get the best shots of seniors and their parents. Host a Spring Graduation Banquet. Following the meal, present the edited year-in-review (complete with sound track and canned laughter). Be sure to budget for this worthwhile venture.

(24) BELIEVE IT OR ELSE!

Have a friendly debate on the "gray areas" of the Christian life, such as the use of leisure time, choices of music, dating, social drinking and dancing. Combine a few teens and parents on each side of the debate. At least three aims come out of this activity: kids and adults both hear a wide range of positions on gray areas; they're able to match a person in their church who holds each particular position; and —most importantly —teens (but also some adults) begin the process of faith ownership. They must ask, "What is it that **I** believe?"

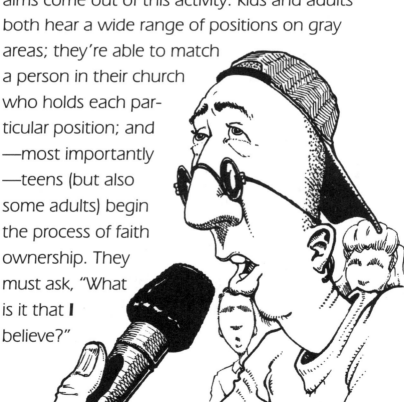

(25) INSTALL HOT LINES

Utilize technology and professionalism to your advantage. Implement a youth group hot line. Some of them are simple, pre-recorded deals. They tell the time and place of the next youth gathering. They can also handle semi-emergencies, like informing callers that there's no ski trip next week because there's not enough snow, and so on. On a more sophisticated level, some youth groups are starting to do hot-line counseling. They've enlisted paid professionals from the church or larger community who volunteer a few hours on the weekend. Parents can call in and talk about their problems. Everybody wins with this ministry.

SAY "PLEASE" AND "THANK YOU"

One of the most significant—yet simple—ways to build a partnership with parents and other adults is to drop them a thank-you note. Thank those who have helped out by cooking, driving, hosting, praying or giving. It's fast. It's inexpensive. And it's thoughtful.

One caution: don't say "thank you" **with a hook attached.** I [Ron] had an experience that illustrates this point. One day, I decided to send out a few notes of appreciation. Among others, I mailed a card to Theresa. She was a single woman who had just finished her first year as the volunteer director of the new junior high group. Two days later, I received a phone call. "I can't believe what you did!" the excited voice on the other end said. It was Theresa. "What do you mean?" I said, half-defensively. "You sent me a thank-you, without a hook!" the teen leader declared, then explained: "You sincerely thanked me for the job I had done.

But you **didn't** add—as so often is the case with these kind of notes—'Can we count on you again next year?' That's a hook. Taking advantage of the situation. Manipulation. Thanks for **not** adding that last part."

㉗ SPEAK FROM THE PULPIT

Encourage your pastor to preach a sermon or two about adolescents. Ask him to address teens themselves, along with their parents. Suggest that he also bring in the larger congregation, too. For example, what responsibilities does the church have to its teens? And vice versa. Go public with your teen ministry. This can be a great recruitment tool for adding healthy adults to your ministry team.

28 USE THE "BUDDY SYSTEM"

Match up "experienced" parents (adults who've had teens in their house for a few years and have lived to talk about it) with "inexperienced" caregivers (parents of pre-teens). During more formal gatherings, members of the former group can offer nuggets of wisdom for the latter. Use panel presentations. Informally, there may be a need for some people to pair up with adults from both groups.

This "buddy" (or mentoring) system could encourage newcomers, offer insights concerning "what you might expect from your new teen" and introduce preteen parents to various support systems that are available, such as vocational guidance counselors at school and driver's training information.

(29) CREATE A "MEN 4 BOYZ" EVENT

This is a father-son night. Do something active like broomball. Rent out an ice rink, put on your tennis shoes, and play hockey with sticks—or brooms—and an old volleyball. Have fathers play against their sons. It's a riot! What happens for those kids that don't have fathers? Or their fathers won't come? Tell them to "adopt a father for the night." Invite other men from your church to participate. The adults will probably have to take the initiative to invite the "fatherless" guys to come with them. It's amazing what this type of contact does for father and son alike.

30 PUT OUT THE WELCOME MAT

Looking for something really easy? Invite parents and other adults to some of the youth events. You can do this through a personal invitation. Send out a letter or put an announcement in your church's newsletter, saying: "For the next few weeks, we want to invite you to youth group. You don't have to cook; you don't have to do anything. Just come, enjoy and be a part of it."

You'd be surprised that some potential volunteers for your youth team might go public because of that night. But, regardless of who signs up, your invitation to these adults will still be grand—because you're building community; you're encouraging generations to talk to each other; you're just being the "church."

31 Do a Dudettes Evening Extravaganza

What's this? A mother-daughter event. Maybe they're into broomball, maybe a bridal or fashion show, or perhaps a "pamper yourself

night." This might include such things as skin care, makeup tips, manicures and hairstyling. You might even want to bring in a skin-care specialist, a cosmetologist or someone who could help them identify "their colors." Ask your females what they prefer. Whatever the choice, the key is that it promotes healthy bonding. Again, include other women (non-mothers of teens) to strengthen the larger fellowship.

If you really feel adventuresome, switch the roles around and plan a father-daughter event (a dance or a banquet) or a mother-son activity, such as a western night or a date with mom (going to a restaurant or concert).

BE RESOURCEFUL

Invest in a resource library for parents and other adults who want to be "in the know" about youth. There are several ways to begin this ministry. The simplest, most straightforward approach is to ask people in the church, "Would you donate $10, $15 or $25 so we can start a library which deals with adolescent issues?" Or, you could try a matching gifts approach where the church budget contributes the same amount that an individual gives. Or, you might just want to take donations of actual books, magazines and videos to loan out to interested adults. The bottom line is that it gets everyone on the same page of youth ministry.

33 CELEBRATE GOOD TIMES (C'MON)

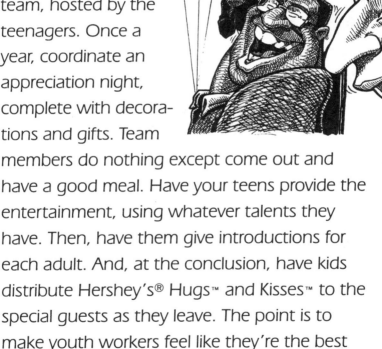

Have a thank-you night for all adults on your leadership team, hosted by the teenagers. Once a year, coordinate an appreciation night, complete with decorations and gifts. Team members do nothing except come out and have a good meal. Have your teens provide the entertainment, using whatever talents they have. Then, have them give introductions for each adult. And, at the conclusion, have kids distribute Hershey's® Hugs™ and Kisses™ to the special guests as they leave. The point is to make youth workers feel like they're the best thing in the world—which they are! For parent appreciation dinners, give them our book, Down-But-Not-Out Parenting.

34 "SAY A LITTLE SOMETHING"

Every month or so, recruit certain parents or other key adults to share their testimonies with the teens, during the youth program. Give them a few hints, such as: "Be honest, but tactful. Share something of your own adolescent years, if appropriate. Talk about the Lord's work in your life. Provide one or two pieces of advice, based on your own experience. Pray about what to say."

A brief Q & A time could follow these testimonies. Don't limit these testimonies to just the parents of teens, or even to adults who are the same age as a teen's parents. Encourage intergenerational exchange.

Such testimonies do much more than provide youth with insights into adults' lives or serve as potential models for them in the church. When I [Ron] employed this strategy, quite often speakers would confess, afterwards: "I truly enjoyed myself. I'm really pleased to see this ministry from this perspective. Now, I'm more aware of some of their needs. I'm able to pray more intelligently."

BRIDGE THE GENERATION GAP

Hold an adult-teen panel discussion. Say you're doing a Sunday school series on understanding teenagers. Or, a youth group series on understanding adults. Invite three or four adults to sit on a panel. Perhaps have one of the teens act like Phil Donahue, or another talk-show host. Referee a debate. And bring in the audience, too. You may want to do this in an evening church service for all to see.

Adults see a new side of teenagers and their world, and vice versa. Just throw out an opening question like: "What's one thing you wish adults would **never** do?" or, "What's the most difficult task of understanding teens?" Use your imagination and enjoy the fun!

36 PLAN AN "OLDIE-BUT-GOODIE NIGHT"

Go back in time, but not quite to the pre-historic era. Plan an evening of nostalgia. Play music from the years when adults were teenagers. Have everyone dress up like they did when they were adolescents—if they can still fit into their clothes! Encourage them to bring old pictures, yearbooks, records and other memorabilia. How about a sock hop complete with a soda fountain that serves ice-cream floats? Talk it up. Do it right. Your young people will think it's a hoot.

37 INVOLVE THE C.I.A.

C.I.A. means **"Caught In the Act** of doing something good." For example, a leader might reward a teen for being polite to someone. Ask yourself, "Where could C.I.A.'s be found in my youth group?"

Katie was the shyest girl in the whole church. One day she got up and performed in a sensational skit. Later that evening, Katie's youth pastor called her mom. He said, "Gwen, you should have seen Katie! Tonight, your daughter got up and startled everyone with her brilliant performance! Good talking to you. Bye." Click. Katie's mom was beside herself. She was probably thinking, "What was **that** all about? Why did he call me? Did he want something? He wants money, doesn't he?" But, seriously, all of a sudden you become an ally, an advocate and encourager of Katie's parents. And what parent doesn't want to hear about his or her kid in such a positive way? It's a win-win situation.

Make C.I.A.'s a churchwide deal. Include one name in each Sunday's bulletin, bring the honored teen on stage and recognize him or her before the assembly.

Test the Barometric Pressure of Your Group

Single out parents and other adults who are aware of and particularly empathetic towards others. Have them keep the youth leaders regularly posted on the "highs" and "lows" in your youth community. These represent "atmospheric conditions" that unwittingly shape your group. These conditions often go undetected by the general public—simply because they're based on private (or semiprivate) experiences.

"Highs" include teen awards at school and other accomplishments; "lows" reflect teenage stress from factors like parents' failing health, divorce or job loss.

PRAY WITHOUT CEASING—
WELL, ALMOST

A few years ago, in Ohio, I [David] asked
four or five parents, "Would you pray regularly
for the youth group and their needs?" They
agreed and said, "Give us a list of the needs."
This simple beginning eventually caused these
burdened parents to remark, "If we come
together just once a month on a Friday night,
it's not enough. We want to meet every other
week." I affirmed them. And some other
(nonparent) adults joined in the fellowship.
More than three-and-a-half years later, these
folks were still praying every other Friday night
for the youth ministry. How would that make
you feel? Wow! What support! What divine
empowerment! Prayer is what undergirds
ministry.

START AN ADVISORY GROUP

This group can offer fantastic assistance. They can provide an endless number of benefits. Such an advisory group might consist of two parents for each grade that the youth ministry serves. In addition, include interested and competent adults who are **not** parents of teens. For example, what about adults with "empty nests," who have successfully raised their teens? They'd be great!

This advisory group can oftentimes diagnose teen needs. They could identify where future ministry might turn. These folks are there to regularly check the pulse of what's going on. Are you offering too many programs? Are you having too many nights out? Are you not having enough retreats? Too few or too many mission trips? These adults can offer their advice. They provide quality control.

I [David] had an exciting experience with one advisory group. One day they said to each other, "We want to be helpful. We need to do more." I responded, "Like what?" And they replied, "Because our youth group is so big, we feel like we're losing students. They're going out the back door." "Well, what do you suggest?" I asked. In unison they exclaimed, "We need a welcome team." Mike said, "I'll do it!" Then, Jennifer mimicked, "Well, I'll do it, too." And, before I knew it, four or five people had volunteered to become our permanent greeters on Sunday morning. All three services at each main door! And some volunteers didn't even have kids of their own. But they had something better—an overwhelming love for teens!

This group could do more than just "greet." They could pass on information about the youth group. They would be invaluable because they would know everything that was happening with your kids. So, they could say to visitors: "Oh, you're a junior higher. Well, then, you go to the third floor"; or "Oh, you're in senior high. You'll like that group. They're having a retreat in two weeks. Here's a flyer on it."

EXPAND YOUR TEAM

Involve a few parents on your adult volunteer staff. It's not always true, but sometimes your best volunteers are parents. Mavis illustrates this fact. A parent of a sophomore, Audra, Mavis had the best spirit possible—she was teachable. She led a small study group. Her girls became very committed to her, and the feeling was mutual. Eventually, these kids would call **her** when they were having problems, instead of calling the youth pastor.

Oh, there's one further blessing of having parents as volunteers. Mavis hit it off so well with the girls that her daughter would say, "Yeah, my mom is really neat. She actually likes being around teenagers. She's great!" This is yet another example of how to get parents to be your allies.

42 CAN I GET A WITNESS?

Ask a parent or other involved adult to testify (publicly) how the youth ministry has impacted his life. Use an adult Sunday school class or even the morning worship hour for the testimony. Have the speaker focus on teen potential. Let him share his excitement and contagious enthusiasm. Do it the day before your leaders plan the church budget.

43 ⚒ DRAFT "VISION STATEMENTS"

Just as successful businesses need intentional mission statements, so do successful families and churches. Fred, the parent of a teen, recently said to me [Ron]: "Neither my teenage son nor I communicate with each other very well. Yet, I want to help him set the right priorities for his future. What can I do?" One idea is to shift verbal communication to written. Put thoughts down on paper. For example, help adult caregivers and teens create a customized game plan—individualized guidelines for their faith-in-life together. What should it include? In the March 7, 1994 issue of CHRISTIANITY TODAY, Clint Kelly suggests a common vision. He says that households must ask these questions:

- **"Why were we given to each other?"**
- **"Why this particular mix of personalities and temperaments?"**
- **"What special gifts, talents and insights does each family member bring to the table?"**

- **"What are the biblical standards for our success as a family?"**

Answers to these questions, among others, form a rough draft for each family's vision statement. Modify it as necessary. Include two or three other families in the congregation, for accountability. Then, post it in the church lobby for ready reference.

Caution: Don't use this statement as a club —to clobber family members who get out of line. Use it to affirm the dignity of individuals. Your goal should always be to build unity.

44 Do Lunch

Take a parent or another adult team member out for lunch, using the church's budget. Let it be just one more expression of your heart—that they really **do** make a difference.

(45) Help Them Cope

1 [Ron] knew a family who suffered greatly when their teenage son tragically died on a church social. Thankfully, these occasions are rare. But how do we help those who **do** suffer in such ways? Provide suitable resources within the fellowship for these parents, including counselors in the community who might help.

Remember that coping with loss can be based on either **physical loss** (via death), or **psychological loss** (via the "empty nest syndrome") when the last teen leaves for college, military service, goes to work or gets married. Offer ongoing support groups to help at these times. Empathize.

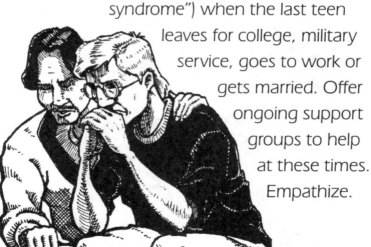

46 SHARE THE LOAD

Distribute surveys to committed adults in your congregation. Discover their skills and interests—even possessions—that they wouldn't mind contributing or loaning to the group. It could be something as simple as letting teens use their house. Or, it could be their willingness to cook, baby-sit or lead a Bible study. Once they sign the forms and turn them in, make sure you follow up. Avoid the mistake of **not** responding to those who say "yes."

 Go It Alone

Take off, with parents only. Hold a retreat. Have a heart-to-heart weekend with them. Allow for spontaneous discussions—or round tables—between a handful of people in each setting. Let parents simply get to know each other. Allow them to get acquainted with other adult team members. This is especially useful at the start of the school year, so that newcomers may fit in quickly. Realizing that "there are others out there like me" makes the weekend successful. Set one realistic goal for all: make one new friend on this retreat, and keep in touch during the year.

(48) Teach in Teams

Ask parents as well as other adults to team up and teach a lesson (or two) to teens, where appropriate. Give them "adjunct" teaching

CHRISTIANS IN VOCATION!

status with your "regular" adult trainers. Have them teach either a **biblical** lesson (using a Scripture passage that's been meaningful for them), or a **topical** lesson (featuring a theme of the Christian life).

I [Ron] had positive experiences with some parents (and other adults) who talked to youth about what it was like to be a believer in their chosen vocations. Topics ranged from being a Christian as a homemaker to construction worker to convalescent home administrator. The purpose for all sessions was to help youth see the viability of each profession—how Christians can be "called" to virtually any type of work. And the payoffs for this team-teaching were incredible! The next time that teens saw these adults "outside of class," it was a totally new and positive encounter. They viewed them in a new light—as living, breathing, **real** Christians.

49 SAY IT WITH CHOCOLATES, . . . OR FLOWERS . . . OR . . .

For those really festive times, announce the occasion with something special. Use a singing telegram or candy, for instance, to celebrate prominent anniversaries of adults on the ministry team, a significant job promotion, or extraordinary efforts of various adults in the youth ministry.

50 HOLD EXIT INTERVIEWS

When some teens, parents or other adult team members are going to leave the youth group (for positive or negative reasons), try to interview them. Get their perceptions (pros and cons) of your ministry. Besides assessing the overall work, ask them to provide one piece of advice for adults, parents and teens who will subsequently join the group. Select insights that are most useful and compile them. Distribute your collection to newcomers at an introductory meeting of adult caregivers who join your community team next year.

PART III

A Look in the
Rearview Mirror

TAG-TEAM YOUTH MINISTRY. Not your typical metaphor for youth work, to be sure. Yet, the more you contemplate it, the more it fits. The more sense it makes.

Youth work is hard stuff. You sweat. You grunt. Sometimes, you're down on all fours. Even on your back. Some weeks are so bad, you know you've been squeezed in a vise once or twice!

And yet, it's still worth the fight. The prize of ultimately watching awkward teens emerge into mature adults is worth it all. No question about it.

But it takes a tag-team effort. Nobody can go it alone. Not the individual teen. Not gifted parents. And, in a sense, not even the faith community, on its own. We all need each other. Like the three-legged stool that sits in our corner of the ring, between rounds, **the youth worker relies upon all three of these parts of teen ministry.**

Like a tag team, we draw strength from knowing someone's always behind us while we're in the ring. We gain confidence and hope, knowing we can stretch out our hand for our partner. Any time we need it, help is not far away.

Oh, one final thought, in case you missed the analogy: **the teens are on our side.** They're in our corner. As partners we're matched up against anything and anybody who would oppose our goal: to bring kids to maturity in Christ. To reconcile them. To make them fully whole.

Finally, in the tough times—times when we don't think we can take any more, times when we can't seem to hold on 'til the bell—don't lose sight of the fact that we've already won. In one sense, our lives are just a rerun of a classic movie that ends "happily ever after." Rejoice! The ultimate battle has already been fought. And we're the victors!

Remember: Someone's already gone to the mat for us.

Also available in the "How to Win" series:

This book offers tons of suggestions to help parents effectively communicate with their teenagers. It's timely, practical and easy to read. It would make a great gift for the parents of your teens!

"The thought-provoking snapshots of life with a teen will make parents nod their heads in agreement and turn page after page."
—**Bo Boshers,** Executive Director
Student Impact High School Ministry
Willow Creek Community Church, South Barrington, IL